MYT....

Five Greek Classics

Adapted
by
ERIC COBLE

Dramatic Publishing
Woodstock, Illinois • England • Australia • New Zealand

*** NOTICE ***

IMPORTANT BILLING AND CREDIT REQUIREMENTS

* * * *

Myth Adventures was first produced at The Cleveland Play House in October 1997, directed by Scott Kanoff, set and lights by Michael Roesch. The cast was as follows:

Midas, Narcissus, Daedalus . . . . Timothy Coles
Dionysus, Nysa, Ariadne. . . . . Anja Lee
Silenus, Calliope, Minos . . . . Maryjo Mace Woodburn
Orpheus, Icarus, Zeus. . . . . Matthew Vinci
Echo, Pageboy, Young Athenian . . . . . Elizabeth Schwartz
Hades, Hera, Theseus . . . . Robin Hannenberg

MYTH ADVENTURES
Five Greek Classics

CHARACTERS:

Dionysus — The god of parties and our narrator

KING MIDAS
Pageboys #1 & #2 — Two of the unluckiest servants on Earth
King Midas — Ruler of Phrygia who understands net worths
Silenus — Dionysus' drinking buddy

ORPHEUS
Calliope — A muse; mother to Orpheus
Orpheus — The greatest musician in history
Charon — The boatsman to the Underworld
Cerberus — A three-headed hell-hound
Hades — Ruler of the Underworld
Euridice — The only woman Orpheus has ever loved

Various ghosts and souls of the dead

ECHO AND NARCISSUS
Echo — The most charming nymph you ever met
Nysa — The second most charming nymph you ever met

Narcissus	The most handsome man he'll ever meet
Zeus	King of the gods
Hera	Unhappy queen of the gods

DAEDALUS AND ICARUS

King Minos	The cruel ruler of Crete
Daedalus	The first great architect
Icarus	His son, a not-so-great architect

THESEUS AND THE MINOTAUR

Theseus	The greatest hero Athens ever produced
Aegeus	His weak old father; King of Athens
Young Athenian	A doomed young man
King Minos	Still the cruel ruler of Crete
Ariadne	The tender daughter of Minos

PLACE:
In and around the Mediterranean Sea.

TIME:
From thousands of years ago to this very moment.

PRODUCTION NOTES: *Myth Adventures* can be performed by 5-26 actors (of any sex or ethnic group) playing all the roles (Dionysus can be played by different actors in different scenes using masks). The props and sets should be minimal, using everyday items to create spectacular theatrical effects.

Although the text was refers to standard interpretations of the costumes and props, some liberties may be taken: In the Cleveland Play House Production, for example, Orpheus carried a Walkman instead of a lyre, Hades was a spidery creature in a wheelchair, and Midas ate golden hamburgers and fries. Have fun.

* * * *

Special thanks to Scott Kanoff
for the lyrics to The Incantation.

6

King Midas

SETTING: *A bare stage that will represent various locales along the Mediterranean Sea.*

AT RISE: *Darkness. Dead silence. Then lights come up on DIONYSUS, the God of Revelry. He wears a traditional Greek mask, wildly painted, and flowing robes that may change color and style with each story. He is surrounded by ACTORS frozen in statuesque poses—each from one of the stories to come. DIONYSUS gazes over them all—over us all—then begins chanting (or singing).*

DIONYSUS.
>WHEN THIS CIRCLE WAS MY ALTAR
>I WAS WORSHIPPED BY THEM ALL
>NOW THE SACRED NAME THEY WHISPERED
>ECHOES THROUGH A RUINED HALL
>
>MID THE STONES AND SUNDERED MARBLE
>CAN OUR SLEEPING DEAD REVIVE?
>WILL THE FIRE BE INVOKED NOW?
>IS THE ECSTASY ALIVE?

(The STATUES join in the chant/song, possibly beginning to move as DIONYSUS touches each of them.)

7

ALL.
          DEEDS OF GLORY, ACTS OF ENVY
          NIGHTS OF PASSION, DAYS OF RAGE
          MORTAL FEAR, CELESTIAL JUSTICE
          CONSECRATE OUR ANCIENT STAGE

          LET THE RITUAL BEGIN AGAIN
          FIRST SOMBER AND AUSTERE
          STONE IS COLD BUT HEAT TAKES HOLD
          WHEN GODS DESCEND AND HOVER NEAR

(*Lights change. The STATUES, now very alive, move off-stage, leaving DIONYSUS to approach an AUDIENCE MEMBER.*)

DIONYSUS. I am Dionysus. The god of…fun. The god of the best parties you will ever attend. And the parties that turn ugly. Very ugly. But I do like my pleasures. You can't have too much of a good thing, can you?

(*He snaps his fingers and a drunken old man, SILENUS, twists onto the stage and collapses unconscious.*)

DIONYSUS (*cont'd*). Or can you. Let us ask…King Midas.

(*He exits the stage as two PAGEBOYS march on, followed by KING MIDAS absentmindedly bringing up the rear, counting gold coins. He looks remarkably like Donald Trump. The group almost trips over SILENUS' body. They pause—perplexed—a little frightened. MIDAS continues counting his money, not looking.*)

PAGEBOY #1 *(whispered).* Your Majesty.

MIDAS. 28, 727...28, 728...what?

PAGEBOY #1. There's, ah, there's a body in the rose garden.

MIDAS. 28...what?

PAGEBOY #1. A body. A human body.

MIDAS. Now look what you've done!! Now we have to start from scratch! That's it. You are no longer Number One Pageboy. You're fired. *(To PAGEBOY #2.)* You. Congratulations, you're now— *(Tripping over the body.)* What's this??

PAGEBOY #2. Sir, a body, sir!

MIDAS. Well, clean it up. Suppose Princess Ino dropped by this afternoon?

PAGEBOY #2. Sir, the body appears to be alive, sir!

MIDAS. Stop shouting. Where's the other pageboy? He may have been brainless, but he was quiet. Well, don't just stand there—get this drunken oaf out of my garden.

(SILENUS moans.)

MIDAS *(cont'd).* Oh, never mind, I'll do it. If you want something done right— You, sir. Drunken oaf. Do you have any idea where you are?

SILENUS. Ubb...no...

MIDAS. You are in the royal rose gardens of Phrygia.

SILENUS. Oh.

MIDAS. Do you have any idea who I am?

SILENUS. ...no...

MIDAS. Typical. I am King Midas of Phrygia.

SILENUS. Oh.

MIDAS. And who are you?

SILENUS. Uff. I don't know…

MIDAS. Wonderful. An amnesiac drunkard in the garden. Perfect start to a Monday.

SILENUS. I was…there was a…party—

MIDAS. Nothing like the party we're going to have when you move on, my inebriated friend— *(He's about to physically shove SILENUS along.)*

SILENUS. Ineb…? I was…where's Dionysus?

MIDAS *(freezes)*. Did you say Dionysus?

SILENUS. I think so.

MIDAS. As in Dionysus the god? *(SILENUS nods.)* The same Dionysus who destroyed the King of Thebes? You're with him?

SILENUS. Not anymore…apparently.

PAGEBOY #1. Your Highness, if he's friends with Dionysus—

SILENUS. Friends?? Ha. More like a father. Taught him everything he knows—

PAGEBOY #2. Sir, best course of action would be to treat him kindly, sir!

MIDAS. Stop shouting.

SILENUS. Please.

MIDAS *(to SILENUS)*. You do look familiar. You have no idea who you are?

SILENUS. Si…

PAGEBOY #1. Sidney?

PAGEBOY #2. Salacious?

MIDAS. Silenus?

SILENUS. That's it! By Zeus, that's me! Thank you.

MIDAS. Totally unnecessary, my friend. I'd recognize you anywhere. You're just…plumper and more…odoriferous than I remember you. But any friend of Dionysus is a friend of mine.

(He claps his hands and the PAGEBOYS scamper around to provide all possible comforts—an umbrella, ornate drink and straw, footstool, etc.)

MIDAS *(cont'd)*. Have a seat. Have a drink, food. Anything you want—are you comfortable? Can we get you anything else? Dancing eunuchs?
SILENUS. No! No, please. I'm...fine. Thank you.
MIDAS. So. Friends with Dionysus, eh?
SILENUS. Thick as thieves.
MIDAS. Where, ah, where would the god be right now, anyway?
SILENUS. Right behind you.

(MIDAS and the PAGEBOYS freeze and do a slow turn. Indeed, there stands DIONYSUS, looking like he's on his way to either a party or a gang war. MIDAS falls to his knees. The PAGEBOYS immediately do the same.)

MIDAS *(cont'd)*. Dionysus. What...ahem. What a pleasure, Your...Specialness.
DIONYSUS. Get up, Midas.
PAGEBOY #2. Sir, *King* Midas, sir!
MIDAS. Shh!! Heh, heh. You can call me Midas. All my friends do. And we are friends, are we not, Dionysus, old chum? Right?
DIONYSUS. That depends. Silenus. How have they treated you?

SILENUS. Like a prince. Would you like a drink with a little umbrella?

(DIONYSUS walks up to MIDAS, raises him up and looks him in the face. Pause. And he grins a huge wonderful grin.)

DIONYSUS. Then we are the best of friends, King Midas!!

MIDAS. Thank the gods. Have a seat! Please! Put your feet up! Mi garden es su garden, compadre.

DIONYSUS. Don't mind if I do. My party passed through your charming gardens here last night. Wasn't till an hour ago though, that we realized we lost Silenus.

(MIDAS and PAGEBOYS laugh a little too appreciatively.)

MIDAS. Ha, ha, ha! Lost Silenus. Ha, ha, ha.

DIONYSUS. So. Midas. What can I do for you?

MIDAS. I beg your pardon?

DIONYSUS. For treating my trusted companion here so well. I owe you. What would you like?

MIDAS. Like? Aha. Me?

DIONYSUS. No, your jolly pageboys here. Of course, you! You're the king, aren't you?

MIDAS. Yes. Yes, I suppose so.

DIONYSUS. So name it. How can I repay you?

MIDAS. I can have anything?

DIONYSUS. I'm a god.

PAGEBOY #1 *(whispered)*. Your Majesty. Please be careful.

PAGEBOY #2 *(trying to whisper)*. Sir, sounds like one of those god tricks, sir.

MIDAS. But I can have anything.

PAGEBOY #2. Sir, I've never heard of anyone coming out happier after one of these transactions, sir.

PAGEBOY #1. Just choose carefully, sire.

MIDAS *(to DIONYSUS)*. Well. I've always loved gold.

DIONYSUS. Money? You just want more money?

MIDAS. No, not just the monetary value, but the color, the glitter, the texture under my fingers, the unmistakable clink of gold on gold as the coins slide through your hands—

DIONYSUS. And you want it all.

MIDAS. I want it now!

DIONYSUS. How much?

PAGEBOY #1. Sire—

MIDAS. A never-ending supply—

PAGEBOY #2. Sire—

MIDAS. Everything I touch! Wherever my fingers lay I'll have gold!!

DIONYSUS. King Midas, do you not have enough gold?

MIDAS. No! There's no such thing!

DIONYSUS. I urge you to reconsider—

MIDAS. You said "anything"! I could have anything— well, that's what I want—gold gold gold in everything I touch!!

(Pause.)

DIONYSUS. So be it.

(Pause.)

MIDAS. That's it? Don't you have to snap your fingers or wink or something?

(DIONYSUS and SILENUS gives each other a look...and burst out laughing.)

DIONYSUS. Silenus. Come on. We've got a party in Egypt.

(SILENUS stumbles up and off.)

MIDAS. But I got my wish, right? You granted my wish?

DIONYSUS. You'll get what you want. But you may not want what you get. *(And he and SILENUS are gone.)*

MIDAS. What did he mean by that? *(The PAGEBOYS look nervously at MIDAS.)* I made a good wish, right? I chose a good power. *(The PAGEBOYS look at each other, trembling.)* So let's test her out. *(He reaches for a small twig with leaves on the ground...hesitates...then touches it. We hear the faint "ch-ching" of a cash register in the distance. MIDAS examines the twig.)* It's...it's gold. I just created a golden leaf. Look! Look! Gold! I made gold!

PAGEBOY #1. Con...congratulations, sire.

PAGEBOY #2 *(quietly)*. Hip, hip...hooray...

MIDAS. Do you realize what this means? No more taxes! No more trade negotiations! I have all the gold I could ever want!! I'm rich! Richer!! The richest man in the world! *(He grabs a rock. Again we hear the cash register "ch-ching.")* Look! A gold nugget! Ha ha ha! Whoo-hoo!!

PAGEBOY #1. Your Majesty—

(MIDAS whips off his sandals—ka-ching!—and goes skipping across the stage to the accompanying register rings.)

MIDAS. Golden blades of grass! Golden grains of sand! Wheee!!! *(He grabs his own face in delight.)*
PAGEBOY #2. Your Highness!!

(A terrified pause as MIDAS realizes he's touching his own skin, then he slowly removes his hands from his cheeks.)

MIDAS. Nothing! Ha! *(Poking himself.)* It's safe! No tricks! Oh, Dionysus, thank you! Thank you! *(He races around touching the floor, the walls of the stage—the cash register ringing like mad.)* Talk about your Midas touch! *(Offering his hand to an AUDIENCE MEMBER.)* King Midas, richest man in the universe. Pleased to meet you. *(Realizing he's about to touch the AUDIENCE's skin, he withdraws.)* Oop. Sorry. Almost forgot. This is the greatest day of my life!!
PAGEBOY #1. I really think Your Highness should be a little careful—
PAGEBOY #2. Yes, Your Majesty, please take care—
MIDAS. Oh, lighten up. Have some blades of grass. *(The PAGEBOYS look at each other, then at MIDAS.)* I mean it. Take it. Sell it. *(He scoops up some twigs and holds them out to the servants.)* A little bonus for keeping this our secret. Go on. Take them. There's more where they came from. *(The PAGEBOYS look at each other again… and dive to the ground, plucking golden blades of grass and grains of sand—stuffing them in pockets, bags,*

wherever they can.) That's the way, boys! Don't be shy! Gold for everyone! Or everyone I like anyway. Ha ha ha! I tell you, my lads, this day— *(unintentionally slaps PAGEBOY #1 on the back. CH-CHING. PAGEBOY #1 freezes)* —is going down in history. One simple act of kindness to a drunken oaf and I...what? *(He notices PAGEBOY #2 staring in horror at his cohort.)* Oh! *(He instinctively jumps back—toward PAGEBOY #2, who screams and scrambles out of the way.)* Wait! Stop! I command you! *(The PAGEBOY stops—cowering at the edge of the stage.)* Let's...just take a breath here. That was a mistake. I need to be more careful. I see that. But...well, this garden needed a new statue, didn't it? And he's in a...lovely pose. So let's...chalk this up to experience and move on. Pageboy?

PAGEBOY #2. Your Majesty?

MIDAS. I think some lunch is in order. All this creation has left me ravenous. Get me food. Now! *(The PAGE-BOY tears off. MIDAS approaches the AUDIENCE and repeatedly almost touches them through the following.)* Look, I'm sorry, all right? I'll send gold to his family. They'll be rich. Happier without him. And he wasn't that good a pageboy, honestly—

(PAGEBOY #2 brings in a tray of food, sets it down, and backs off—way off.)

MIDAS *(cont'd).* So I have to give up shaking hands and hugging and—well, touching another human being in any way ever again. But look at all this gold! Who needs personal relationships when you can buy brilliant long-distance conversations? *(He formally sits down—*

prepares to eat—takes a piece of bread—ch-ching—and brings it to his mouth... Crunch. Solid gold. He winces, but covers up his embarrassment. To PAGEBOY.) Ahem. This golden bread is for you. Enjoy. *(He returns to his food—carefully takes a fork—ch-ching—and puts it into another piece of bread. Nothing. He grins and brings the bread to his lips—ch-ching. Crunch. He drops the fork in terror and starts grasping at the other food in every way possible—using the tray, a napkin, lying face down on the floor and gnawing at the bread...all of it results in golden, inedible food.)* No. No, no, no— *(He grabs his goblet—ch-ching—takes a fast swig of water—ch-ching—and spits out the golden undrinkable mess.)* No!! I'll starve! I'll die of thirst! What kind of trick is this??

PAGEBOY #2 *(weakly).* Respectfully, sir, no trick, sir, it's what you asked for...sir.

MIDAS. What good is all the gold in the universe if I'm going to die in a week?

PAGEBOY #2. Is that a real question, sir?

MIDAS. Not to you. To Dionysus. What are you trying to do?? I asked for a simple wish— I didn't think that you'd...that I'd— *(Falling to the ground and banging his fists with the accompanying ch-chings.)* No! No! No! I'm a fool! Stupid, stupid fool! What was I thinking? I was greedy, I'm sorry. Dionysus, I'm sorry, just take this away! Save me, Dionysus! *(Reaching for the PAGEBOY who recoils.)* Stupid, stupid, stupid—

(DIONYSUS appears behind MIDAS.)

DIONYSUS. Yes.

MIDAS. Dionysus! *(Reaching for the god, who raises a warning finger.)* I'm so sorry. You were right. I have enough gold, I'll never ask for more again, please, just take back your gift, please, please—

DIONYSUS. Go. Wash yourself in the River of Pactolus that runs beside Sardis. You'll lose your fatal gift.

MIDAS. Thank you. Thank you!! *(He charges off and re-enters almost immediately from the opposite side of the stage.)*

DIONYSUS. That was fast.

MIDAS. I was motivated. *(He grabs up a twig...Nothing.)* Ha! Oh, wondrous! To hold a twig. *(Grabbing a handful of bread and stuffing it into his mouth.)* Ummm-brrgd. Glommurus, glommurs brrgd. *(Swallowing.)* Thank you, Dionysus, thank you! I've changed my ways. You'll see. I've changed! *(And he dances offstage.)*

DIONYSUS *(looks at PAGEBOY #2)*. I think you'll find that from this day on, there will be gold in the River Pactolus. Free for the taking.

(PAGEBOY #2's eyes light up. He charges toward the river.)

DIONYSUS *(cont'd., to AUDIENCE)*. No, you can never have too much of a good thing— *(He gently pats the frozen golden PAGEBOY.)* ...can you?

(DIONYSUS stands smiling at us...as lights go down to...Blackout.)

Orpheus

(DIONYSUS steps forward.)

DIONYSUS. But have you ever wanted something so badly, that you could think of nothing, nothing, nothing else? It filled your every thought—your every dream—something you would do anything—*anything*—to get? Well, meet Orpheus.

(ORPHEUS, a sweet-looking young man, enters playing an abstract lyre. We hear the beautiful music.

EURIDICE enters opposite—a beautiful young woman. They slowly cross on parallel lines as DIONYSUS weaves between them.)

DIONYSUS *(cont'd)*. This was Orpheus whose mother the muse left him the greatest gift: music. This was Orpheus whose melodies would draw trees to lean over him and listen; leaves and streams to grow quiet and hear his melody. This was Orpheus who sailed with Jason and the Argonauts, whose music overcame the evil songs of the Sirens. This was Orpheus who faced beasts and demons and journeyed thousands of miles...to seek a love as deep as his music. And this is Orpheus who found Euridice.

(The couple stop on opposite corners of the stage and face each other. They move toward one another as if in a marriage ceremony.)

DIONYSUS *(cont'd)*. Love at first sight—two souls entwining as one—and the melodies of Orpheus soared higher and swooped deeper than ever before. The earth itself rose up to watch the lovers on their wedding day… but the Fates were weaving a different tapestry—

(The couple are almost in an embrace…the music echoing…trance-like…through the space.)

DIONYSUS *(cont'd)*. A venomous snake lay in the grass that day beneath Euridice's feet—

(ORPHEUS moves to hold her…but the dark shadow of cloaked HADES moves in and swallows her up.)

DIONYSUS *(cont'd)*. And as the poison coursed through her blood, their day of marriage became a day of devastation.

(ORPHEUS slowly collapses to the ground.)

DIONYSUS *(cont'd)*. And Orpheus never—*never*—recovered. *(DIONYSUS exits.)*

(Pause.

ORPHEUS lays crumpled where he fell. Then in glides CALLIOPE, a woman of undetermined age—a muse.)

CALLIOPE. Orpheus?

ORPHEUS. Mother.

CALLIOPE. She is the one who died. Not you.

ORPHEUS. We both died on that day. But she was able to travel to the Underworld, while I am still chained to this realm where every hour is another stone laid on my chest.

CALLIOPE. You take no food...you take no drink—

ORPHEUS. Nothing can fill the pit she's opened up.

CALLIOPE. Your music...use your music—

ORPHEUS. Will it bring her back? Can a sweet tune raise the dead?

CALLIOPE. If there is any song that can perform such a feat, it is yours, my son.

ORPHEUS. Could it truly?

CALLIOPE. You were given a tremendous gift, Orpheus. If you now keep it locked within you, then not only will Euridice have died, but the music that brings life to future generations will never be born.

ORPHEUS. Pretty thoughts. But useless. I can't play without her. If part of us dies because of that, then so be it. I didn't put the viper in her path. Go ask your gods why they would deprive the world of music.

CALLIOPE. I am asking you.

ORPHEUS. And I'm asking you how I can get her back. Don't you think I want to sing? Do you think I ever knew any peace when I wasn't creating music? But I need Euridice. I didn't know it until I found her, but now I need her, I can't think, I can't breathe, I can't... do...anything! How do I get her back? Tell me!

CALLIOPE. I cannot help you.

ORPHEUS. But you know of a way?

CALLIOPE. Orpheus, heed me, look within yourself—heal your own wounds—

ORPHEUS. Mother, I'm begging you. I'm already dying— if there's a chance—any chance of finding her...tell me.

(Pause.)

CALLIOPE. I know of the entrance to a cave. There begins the treacherous pathway to the Underworld. The realm of Hades, Brother of Zeus and Poseidon. Hades, lord of the dead. If he has taken her, then that is where you will find her.

ORPHEUS. Show me this cave.

CALLIOPE. You are mortal. You will find it soon enough.

ORPHEUS. Show me this cave.

CALLIOPE. Orpheus, no one returns from that dread place. There are too many tortures, too many traps—

ORPHEUS. Mother. I will have Euridice. Show me this cave.

(Pause as ORPHEUS and CALLIOPE stare hard at each other, then CALLIOPE spins away and a shaft of light shines down on ORPHEUS. The rest of the stage goes dark. He is blinded. Pause.)

ORPHEUS. Mother?

(A quiet dripping of water is heard. ORPHEUS steps out into the darkness. He moves from one pool of light to another—each a different hue and intensity. He grows tired, but still driven...then lights come up on a blood-red cloth laying across his path.)

ORPHEUS. The River Styx.

(Two ACTORS in black enter and raise the cloth—gently rippling it to create the water. Then from behind the red—rising out of it—appears CHARON, the hooded ferryman. We cannot see his face or hands, and when he speaks it is in an echoing whisper.)

CHARON. Sssseek you passage through the land of the dead?

ORPHEUS. I come seeking my bride. Are you not Charon, the boatsman who ferries souls to the underworld?

CHARON. Your body still clings to you. I offer no passage.

ORPHEUS. I can pay. More than the paltry coins you take from the mouths of the dead. Just take me across.

CHARON. Ssssouls.

ORPHEUS. You can have my soul! I must cross the River Styx!

(He charges toward CHARON, who raises a hand to halt him...and we see the crumbling bones of CHARON's fingers. ORPHEUS freezes—wracked with pain.)

CHARON. It is not your time. Turn back.

(ORPHEUS buckles with the pain...then strains to play a note on his lyre...a beautiful chord that hangs in the air...CHARON pauses.)

CHARON *(cont'd)*. What is it you do?

ORPHEUS *(regaining some of his strength)*. Music…
(Plays another chord—gaining more strength.) I give
you my music.

*(CHARON lowers his hand completely as ORPHEUS
plays on.)*

CHARON. Ssssail with me, Orpheus. Play your melody
and I grant you passage.

*(The river lowers and ORPHEUS steps onto the "boat"
with CHARON, who proceeds to steer them over. The
river grows calmer and calmer—the lights growing dimmer and dimmer as ORPHEUS' lovely song echoes
through the space.*

The water stops and ORPHEUS steps from the boat.)

CHARON. Ccccerberusss. The three-headed dog at the
gate of Hadesss. Beware him, Orpheusss. He may not
care for your musssic. And walk with the dead, not
through them. *(CHARON steps back into the shadows
and disappears.)*

*(ORPHEUS stops playing and looks around. Silence. He
steps into the darkness… Another step… RROOAARRR!!
CERBERUS—the huge hell-hound—lunges forward—its
snarling body and heads made up of three ACTORS in
masks. It slams ORPHEUS backward. He rolls out of the
way of a second lunge—the howling, rabid monster
spins to face him—teeth gnashing—about to rip his
throat out…and ORPHEUS plays. He plays a simple*

quiet tune as calmly as he can...the dog freezes—or rather two heads do; the third keeps straining to snap at him. ORPHEUS continues.)

ORPHEUS. Good dog. Good Cerberus.

(CERBERUS whines, cocks his heads and backs off— then forward—checking out this intruder, but unwilling to press the attack.)

ORPHEUS *(cont'd).* Sit.

(CERBERUS does—almost lying down.

ORPHEUS plays on—backing away—and looks up at a looming portal.)

ORPHEUS *(cont'd).* So these are the gates of Hades. Thank you, Cerberus.

(The hell-hound whines and thinks about rolling over.

ORPHEUS steps away as CERBERUS fades into the darkness. The young musician keeps playing this time... stepping farther...looking in all directions...when we hear faintly in the distance—very faintly, but growing louder—a plaintive howl—coming from all directions... ORPHEUS looks around—not sure where to move—the howl is now deafening...then in swoop the GHOSTS OF THE DEAD—what seem like thousands of them— cloaked and ragged—unrecognizable as human beings— lights careening around— They tear at ORPHEUS—who is buffeted by them—with them.)

GHOST #1. Help us, Orpheus—
ALL *(echoing)*. Help us…help us…
ORPHEUS. Who are you?
GHOST #2. We are ghosts—
GHOST #3. Souls of the dead…
GHOST #1. Trapped in the Underworld…
ORPHEUS. What can I do—
GHOST #1. Save us…
GHOST #2. Save us…
GHOST #3. Save us…
GHOST #2. Take us back with you…
GHOST #3. Free our souls…
ORPHEUS. I cannot.
GHOST #1. But your power…
GHOST #2. Your music…
GHOST #3. Your power…
GHOST #1. Can free us…
ORPHEUS *(trying to break free)*. I cannot save you. I am
    here for one woman—she is all I can save!

*(And ORPHEUS releases and flows with them instead of
fighting them.)*

GHOST #3. Then you will stay with us…
GHOST #2. Ease our pain…
GHOST #1. Play your music forever…
GHOST #2. Here…
GHOST #3. Here…
ALL. Here…

(ORPHEUS is now lost—struggling to keep playing.)

ORPHEUS. I cannot—let me go—I cannot save you! I will not save you—you have no power...over me—let me go!

(And he is thrown to the ground. Total stillness. He's alone. Silence. Then we hear the ghostly voices echoing offstage.)

GHOST #1. Then you face Hades...alone.
GHOST #2. Alone.
GHOST #3. Alone.

(The voices fade away.

Again, silence. ORPHEUS peers into the darkness...and hears a giant iron door grinding open.

...and from the darkness emerges HADES, god of the Underworld, inching forward like a spider, twisted.)

HADES *(in a broken voice)*. Mortal. Who. Are. You.

(ORPHEUS kneels, fighting his instinct to run like a rabbit.)

ORPHEUS. I am called Orpheus. And I seek—
HADES. I know what you seek. I am a god.
ORPHEUS. Of course. May I have Euridice then? *(HADES laughs.)* Did I say something humorous?
HADES. You think a simple request can bring someone back from the dead?
ORPHEUS. The mere fact that I ventured into your realm should show you—

HADES. That you are a fool. Think for a moment, Orpheus. If I grant your plea—give you your wife back—everyone who ever lost anyone—a son, a mother, the friend of a friend, a dear pet—would come slithering down here to fetch them back. There would be less peace in death than in life. This is not a revolving door. This. Is. The Underworld. You have violated the very laws of nature. And for that you must pay the price. *(He raises his gnarled hands.)*

ORPHEUS. Wait. I offer you one gift. To make amends for disturbing your kingdom. *(He begins the simplest, loveliest tune we have yet heard.*

(HADES pauses...lowers his arms.)

ORPHEUS *(quietly as he plays)*. Your Lordship. You alone rule over everyone. No one escapes your reach. Kings and beggars will live side by side in your domain. But I ask you. My wife—my one love—was taken too soon. Her flowers had yet to bloom and you tore her from me. I don't ask for much. Just for her. For what will only be a few moments in your eternity. Just until her natural years fade away. Then she—and I—will return, never to trouble you again. I ask not that you *give* her to me. But lend her. What shall be yours shall be yours. Please. *(He stops playing and looks up at HADES.)*

(Pause.)

HADES *(reaching up and touching his own cheek)*. Hah. An iron tear. Your song is truly magical, Orpheus. I cannot deprive the world of such beauty. Yet. Go. Take your wife.

ORPHEUS. Thank you, Your Lordship.

HADES. Turn and leave my kingdom the way you entered. Euridice shall follow you out. But if you ever turn back to face her—if you look at her in any way before you reach the daylight at the mouth of the cave...she is mine. And will be forever lost to you.

ORPHEUS. Your Majesty, thank you. Thank you. *(He turns and takes a deep breath...and heads out.)*

(HADES fades back into the darkness and we hear a huge iron door shutting with an eerie finality.

ORPHEUS re-enters in the dimness. A cloaked FIGURE glides in silently behind him. He does not ever turn to face her.)

ORPHEUS. Euridice? Are you there? *(Silence.)* Euridice. It is I. Orpheus. I came for you. Can you not speak my name? *(Silence. ORPHEUS takes several steps...and pauses.)* I know you're there. We'll be free soon.

(He moves on. The FIGURE follows him.

The red cloth appears again—as does CHARON and his boat.)

CHARON. Sssso, mortal. You sssurvived Cerberusss and the ssssouls of the dead...

ORPHEUS. They were not even visible on my way back. As if they'd all been commanded to step aside.

CHARON. Sssso we have. And now you return to your own world.

ORPHEUS. I do. But not alone. There are two of us to ferry across the Styx, are there not?

(CHARON merely gestures to climb aboard. ORPHEUS does. So does the shadowy FIGURE. CHARON begins to row.)

ORPHEUS. Why do I feel no extra weight on the boat? Charon, is there someone following me or not? *(CHARON steers on, silently.)* I just...if this is a trick by Hades...he can't...I won't— *(CHARON docks the boat and the red cloth slithers away.)* Thank you. *(He steps out. So does the FIGURE. CHARON fades away.)* I'll see you again soon. *(Beat.)* Let's start walking, shall we? *(He moves from pool of light to pool of light, occasionally stopping abruptly, attempting to catch some sound from behind him. He never does.)* It's much harder to climb than it was to descend. Don't you agree? Almost there, I think. Why does he not want me to see your face? He hasn't...done anything to you, has he? They say you enter the Underworld looking exactly as you left this one...so I don't suppose you'd look any less...beautiful. Almost there. *(Stopping.)* I'm sorry you were alone in the field. I keep thinking if I'd been with you I would've seen the snake, our voices laughing would have frightened it away, that I could have...done something. So I'm doing something now. I've come for you. *(Climbing farther, the FIGURE following.)* My music finally achieved something real. Not just a tune that lives only in the memory, but something you can feel and touch— Almost there. Why can't you speak? I know the gods twist the wishes they grant...but he promised—Euridice. I think I see light. The entrance... we're there. I see the sunrise! We're...almost...there— *(Nearing the entrance.)* Euridice. We're free.

(He steps into the light—turns to embrace her...but she is still in the darkness. She throws off her cowl to reveal her beautiful sad face...as a great howl begins in the distance...)

ORPHEUS. No...
EURIDICE *(almost whispered)*. Farewell...

(The GHOSTS come shrieking up and around her—pulling her back into blackness... ORPHEUS stands with his hands outstretched.)

ORPHEUS. Nooo!! *(Silence. He collapses.)*

(DIONYSUS steps forward from the darkness.)

DIONYSUS *(to AUDIENCE)*. Orpheus died shortly thereafter and rejoined his love in the Underworld, where I suppose he plays his songs to this day. Easing the suffering of those he left behind...and who left him behind. The gods do grant wishes. In their way.

(Blackout.)

Echo and Narcissus

(Silence. Then onto the stage explodes ECHO, a charming young woman who races up to the AUDIENCE— shaking hands, giggling, and above all, talking.)

ECHO. Oh, hello, how do you do—hello, up there—enjoying the show? Wasn't that Orpheus thing sad? I mean, I love music, but to go into Hades— I used to play, you know—trombone—does anyone here play trombone—or any instrument? Tambourine, anyone? And I love woodwinds—

(DIONYSUS enters.)

ECHO *(cont'd)*. Dionysus! Hello, sweetie! *(Kissing his cheek.)* Oh, it's been too long—how are you? How was Thebes?

DIONYSUS *(to AUDIENCE)*. In case you think the gods are only cruel to mortals, think again. They can be just as...temperamental...with each other—

ECHO. Oh, I know. The whole Prometheus thing—that was just awful—chained to a rock for eternity with a buzzard pecking out your liver every morning! Talk about a rude wake-up call—

DIONYSUS. There was once a lesser group of goddesses known as "nymphs"—a group of lovely young ladies—

ECHO. Oh, now—

DIONYSUS. The most famous of whom was Echo.

ECHO. That would be me. Not to brag, but my parties are always the smash of the season on Olympus—you can hear the thunderclaps for miles around—

DIONYSUS. But her last encounter with the gods was not such a pleasant one. *(He kisses her cheek and leaves.)*

ECHO. Not such a...what do you mean, Dionysus? I've always had excellent times—just last week, Hephaestes—what do you mean?

(NYSA, another nymph, strides on.)

ECHO. Oh! Nysa! Everyone, this is Nysa. We went to nymph school together and she is my dearest, closest, dearest best friend in the whole entire globe.

NYSA. Mm. Lovely day, isn't it, Echo, darling? I was thinking of going dancing with the satyrs a little later, want to come?

ECHO. Love to, love to! I just need to trim my— *(Looking offstage.)* Oh. Oh! Oh!! Look! Looklooklooklook—

NYSA. Is that who I think it is?

ECHO. It is. It is it is it is!

NYSA. Oh! Get ready!

(They scramble into alluring poses.)

ECHO. But don't look like you're getting ready.

(They go nonchalant.)

NYSA. But look interested.
ECHO. But busy with something else.

(They are totally flustered.)

NYSA. Just—
NYSA & ECHO. Act casual! *(They throw themselves into achingly casual poses.)*

(And in walks NARCISSUS, a devastatingly handsome young man, striding across the stage with his bow and arrows—eyes straight ahead, chin held high—exuding the kind of confidence self-help books can only dream of.)

ECHO. Ahem.
NYSA. Oh. Hello, Narcissus.
ECHO. Narcissus? Oh! I didn't hear you approaching.

(He doesn't even turn to look at them—just keeps striding.)

NYSA. Lovely day, isn't it?
ECHO. We were just thinking of going dancing later, Narcissus, would you—

(He stops. Lets out a deep sigh of aggravation.)

NYSA. —not that you would have to dance…you could just—
ECHO. —stand around—
NYSA. —if you want. Or…dance…or…how are you?

NARCISSUS *(not facing them)*. You're in love with me. I know you're in love with me. Everybody is in love with me. If we could somehow build a relationship on a foundation of trust and no physical attraction whatsoever, perhaps I could speak to you. But obviously you are too enmeshed in your own co-dependent neediness which you mistakenly label "love" to allow me space to share my inner feelings and thoughts intimately with you. So please. Don't talk to me. Thank you. *(He strides off.)*

(Pause.)

ECHO. What?

NYSA. We were too obvious.

ECHO. "Co-dependent whatiness"?

NYSA. He's like that with everyone. Don't take it personally.

ECHO. But we're nymphs. Everyone loves a nymph.

NYSA. There are other fish in the Mediterranean Sea. Believe me.

ECHO. But he's the handsomest, ravest, most confident fish I've ever not met.

NYSA. It's called hubris, honey. He'll get his.

(A huge thunderclap and lightning flash behind them. ECHO and NYSA keep staring after NARCISSUS.

Then in walks ZEUS, in a flashy leisure suit looking like a mid-life crisis in full bloom.)

ZEUS. Hey, babes!

ECHO & NYSA *(not turning to face him)*. Oh. Hey, Zeus.

ZEUS. Just when I thought the day couldn't get any more gorgeous, I see you two. I didn't know they made goddesses this beautiful anymore.

NYSA *(calmly turning to face him)*. How are you today, Zeus?

ZEUS. What. Aren't you glad to see me?

NYSA. Sure.

ZEUS. "Sure." "How are you today, Zeus?" Is that any way to greet the King of the Gods?

NYSA. We were just discussing something. Girl talk.

ECHO. We're still glad to see you.

NYSA. Sure.

ZEUS. Good. Thought I might be losing my touch. What say we go for a stroll down by the creek?

NYSA. Mm. What if Hera sees us?

ZEUS. Hera?

ECHO. Your wife? She was pretty ticked that last time. Remember that whole bull thing?

ZEUS. Yes, yes, yes. Well, we have an understanding. She's much less jealous these days. Besides, she's out hunting with Artemis today. Come on. A little strollsy-wollsy with Zeusy-goosey?

ECHO. Ooo. Poetry. How can we resist?

NYSA. I'll come with you, Zeus.

ZEUS. Echo?

ECHO. No thanks. I'll wait here. Just in case...someone comes along who I...need to see or say hello to—

NYSA. Bird in the hand, honey.

(She and ZEUS head off.)

ZEUS. You like birds? Have I ever shown you my swan trick?

(And they're gone.)

ECHO. See you. Hope Hera doesn't—

(In storms HERA, a woman on a rampage.)

ECHO *(cont'd)*. Hera! Oh dear, hi! Hi! How are you? How's Artemis?

HERA. Out of my way, nymph. I'm looking for my no-good, two-timing, double-crossing, back-stabbing, cross-dealing, boot-licking husband. Have you seen him?

ECHO. Um...why?

HERA. If I catch him strolling with another woman one more time, I will single-handedly tear him—and her— limb from limb from limb with my bare teeth!!

ECHO. Ah. No. Haven't seen him.

HERA. Then step aside. Goddess coming through.

(She heads in the direction ZEUS and NYSA left, but ECHO leaps in her way.)

ECHO. Wait! Um. How's the Trojan War going? I heard that ever since you sided with the Greeks, they've been tromping Troy like nobody's—

HERA. I have no time for—

(HERA continues her attempts to get past, ECHO gracefully stopping her.)

ECHO. And the whole Trojan horse idea! Was that yours? You know, I had a wooden horse when I was little— I mean, nowhere near the size of the Trojan one, but—

HERA. Echo—

ECHO. I mean, I'm just so in awe of a woman who steps up and protects her friends—risking her own life— I just think that's so great—

HERA. If—

ECHO. And speaking of strong women, I don't know if you've talked to Atalanta lately—

HERA. Could—

ECHO. She's in this race this weekend, running for love or something, I think that's so great, don't you?

HERA. I—

ECHO. That's a great toga—where did you get it?

HERA. Echo!!

ECHO. Yes?

HERA. Step. Aside.

ECHO. Ah. Why didn't you say so? Oh, did Aphrodite do your hair? It looks fabulous—

(ZEUS wanders in humming a tune to himself...and sees HERA. He stops dead in his tracks.)

ZEUS. Hera! Sweetie! What a charming surprise! Have you been here long?

HERA. Don't you "sweetie" me, you poor excuse for omnipotence. Where have you been?

ZEUS. Just...strolling.

HERA. Alone?

(NYSA walks in.)

NYSA. Oh! Hera! Um, what a surprise!

(HERA glares at ZEUS.)

ZEUS *(to NYSA)*. Ah. Hello, young lady. I don't believe we've had the pleasure. I'm Zeus. And since I've clearly never met you before in my life, please introduce yourself for the first time to my lovely wife and myself, who as I said, is Zeus. Am Zeus.

NYSA. I think I should be going.

ECHO. Me too. Ciao.

(They dart for an exit.)

HERA. Hold!

(The NYMPHS freeze and turn around.)

HERA *(cont'd)*. Echo. Come here. *(ECHO gestures "me?" HERA nods malevolently and ECHO approaches.)* I may not have caught my husband red-handed, but I know the reason. Your tongue has made a fool of me for the last time.

ECHO. My tongue? My tongue wouldn't hurt a flea, I'd never—

HERA. Always have to have the last word, don't you? Well, henceforth, that's all you ever will have. *(She touches ECHO's throat and holds it. ECHO is terrified. A long moment passes... Then HERA steps away.)* The last word, but never the first. What do you have to say for yourself now, nymph?

ECHO. Say for yourself now, nymph. *(She gasps and grabs her throat—looking to NYSA and ZEUS in alarm.)*
ZEUS. What's wrong?
ECHO. What's wrong!
ZEUS. I'm asking you.
ECHO. I'm asking you!
ZEUS. Are you mocking me?
ECHO. Mocking me?
ZEUS. Listen, young lady—
ECHO. Listen, young lady!
ZEUS. What?? I'm leaving before I let loose with a lightning bolt. Come Hera. Let's go home.
ECHO *(pleading after them).* Go home!
ZEUS. That's what we're doing!
ECHO. What we're doing!
ZEUS. No, what *we're* doing. You can stay here with your own kind.
ECHO *(begging HERA).* Your own kind!

(HERA just smiles at ECHO.)

ZEUS. No, your own kind. Our kind is through with you.

(He and HERA walk off.)

ECHO *(sinking to the ground).* ...through with you... *(Pause. She looks at NYSA. Tries to speak...but can't.)*
NYSA. What?
ECHO. What?
NYSA. What are you looking at?
ECHO. Looking at?

NYSA. Listen, thanks for looking out for Zeus and me. Really. But if Hera's after you...I think maybe it'd be better if we stayed away from each other from now on. All right?

ECHO. All right?

NYSA. Good. Maybe you should just...go live in the woods. Less people there.

ECHO. Less people there—

NYSA. Right! Good idea! You won't be tempted to talk.

ECHO. Tempted to talk?

NYSA. Look, I've gotta run. Take care.

ECHO. Take care.

NYSA. Thanks. See you.

ECHO. See you.

NYSA. Right. *(And she leaves.)*

ECHO *(quietly)*. Right.

(ECHO looks around dejectedly, almost in tears. She wanders off into the woods... Only to almost be run over by NARCISSUS—hunting with his bow. ECHO lights up—ecstatic—she moves for him...then stops herself. He continues hunting—her following his every step—at one point reaching out a hand to touch him...then pulling back. NARCISSUS stops. Looks around.)

NARCISSUS. Wait. Where's the rest of my male-bonding party? I'm lost. Yes, I feel confident enough in my manhood to admit that I'm lost. I have no idea where I am.

ECHO *(stifles a whisper)*. Where I am.

NARCISSUS. What?

(ECHO clamps her mouth shut.)

NARCISSUS *(cont'd)*. Listen, I'm feeling rather vulnerable right now. Is there anybody here?

ECHO *(can't help herself)*. Here! *(He spins to where her voice came from, but she easily dodges out of eyesight, totally embarrassed.)*

NARCISSUS. Who's here?

ECHO. Here!

(Again he pursues and she darts away.)

NARCISSUS. Who are you? Come to me!

ECHO. Come to me!

NARCISSUS. Are you following me?

ECHO. Following me!

NARCISSUS. Stop it! Let us meet!

(Pause. She hesitates...scared...then she steps forward.)

ECHO. Let us meet.

NARCISSUS. Oh no. Not you.

ECHO *(approaching him)*. Not you—

NARCISSUS. Leave me alone!

ECHO *(trying to embrace him)*. Alone!

NARCISSUS *(pushing her away)*. I could never love you.

ECHO *(pauses...then retreating quietly)*. Love you. Love you...

NARCISSUS. I'll die before I give you power over me!

ECHO. I give you power over me.

NARCISSUS *(turning away)*. This is ridiculous. *(Seeing a pool of water.)* I need a drink. *(He kneels.)* I realize I'm just avoiding my problems with this distraction, but I feel...feel... *(Seeing his own reflection.)* Hell-o. *(To the pool.)* Do I know you? I realize it's a cliché—but do you come here often? You're very attractive.

ECHO. Attractive.

NARCISSUS *(to pool).* Your eyes...

ECHO. Your eyes...

NARCISSUS. ...are like...Apollo's fire. Your hair...

ECHO. Your hair...

NARCISSUS. Your lips...

ECHO. Your lips...

NARCISSUS. You're so beautiful.

ECHO. Beautiful.

NARCISSUS. May I kiss you?

ECHO. Kiss you?

(He kisses his reflection and bolts upright, wiping his lips—then sees himself backing away in the pool.)

NARCISSUS. Where are you?

ECHO. Are you?

NARCISSUS. Come back. Please come back.

ECHO. Come back.

NARCISSUS *(again seeing his reflection).* There you are. There.

ECHO. There.

NARCISSUS. I could...

ECHO *(overlapping).* I could...

NARCISSUS. ...look at you...

ECHO. ...look at you...

NARCISSUS. ...forever.

ECHO. Forever.

(DIONYSUS walks out between the two isolated figures.)

DIONYSUS. And so he did. He never left that spot. Narcissus died, drowning in his own reflection. But the gods turned him into a beautiful flower with white petals and a golden center—the kind that still leans over pools of water today. And Echo? She crawled into a cave to hide from the world and just faded away in the darkness. But her voice lives on. The next time you call out in a hollow, it won't be your own voice that answers you. But Echo.

(Blackout. Then from the darkness…)

ECHO *(O.S)*. Echo…echo…

Daedalus and Icarus

(Lights come up on KING MINOS, a vitriolic ruler whose voice would deafen a buffalo.)

MINOS. Where's the architect?? Get him out here! And who gave me these grapes?? They're not round! The King of Crete will not eat these! Where's that architect?? And somebody get me something for this headache! Where in Hades is that architect??

(DAEDALUS enters with ICARUS. DAEDALUS is a quiet, calm man—slightly distracted—always working on something in his mind, and seemingly unimpressed by MINOS. ICARUS is a fidgety young man with hungry eyes.)

DAEDALUS. Here, uh, Your Majesty, I'm—we're here.
MINOS. Who are you??
DAEDALUS. The architect. We're the architect.
MINOS. Both of you? I hired one!
DAEDALUS. Daedalus, Your Royalness. I'm the architect. I suppose. I also paint and sculpt and...the saw? You know? I invented that. And glue. That was mine too. Icarus. This is my son, Icarus. An apprentice, of sorts. Follows me everywhere. Good boy, good boy. You have a monster?

MINOS. You could say that.

(The low rumbling of the MINOTAUR echoes over the stage.)

DAEDALUS. Sounds large.

MINOS. The Minotaur is bigger than three men. A horrible beast. And also my son.

DAEDALUS. Ah. Your what?

MINOS. He's not literally my son, idiot. A few years ago, I...did some things—some miscalculations—and Poseidon cursed my wife to give birth to this...thing. It's half bull and half human. A huge lumbering beast with a taste for human flesh.

DAEDALUS. And this is problematic because—

MINOS. Because I'm not going to kill it! I can't. I won't. But it's eating the guards.

DAEDALUS. And that's problematic because—

MINOS. I'm running out of guards, you fool! I'm looking at a full-scale revolt if I don't do something!

ICARUS *(stepping forward)*. Father—

DAEDALUS. Not now, my boy, not— *(to MINOS)* —and you want me to...contain...the Minotaur?

MINOS. I've heard of your buildings, of your skills. So create something to hold him. It.

(Pause. DAEDALUS ponders...then.)

DAEDALUS. Give me two hours. I'll...we'll contain him.

MINOS. It. I'll make you a rich man, Daedalus. *(Calling offstage as he leaves.)* Where are those grapes? The King of Crete needs his grapes!! *(And he's gone.)*

DAEDALUS. Grapes. A good grape is worth all the riches in— *(He lays out a piece of paper and begins calculating.)*

(ICARUS tries to stand still and watch.)

ICARUS. Father.

(Pause. DAEDALUS is completely absorbed. ICARUS begins wandering around.)

ICARUS *(cont'd)*. I don't like it. I don't trust him. Anyone who would cross paths with Poseidon—

DAEDALUS. Do you have the chalk?

ICARUS *(fishing chalk out of his tunic)*. I want to see this Minotaur.

DAEDALUS. The light. You're blocking it. Move.

ICARUS. Can I help? *(Kneeling beside the paper.)* Are these the walls? *(DAEDALUS keeps working.)* Why is this one shorter than those? Shouldn't they—

DAEDALUS. Icarus.

ICARUS. Sorry. *(Pause.)* What if you put a big steel spike right here?

DAEDALUS. You're in my light again.

ICARUS. Sorry. *(He backs off.)* My mistake. I thought I was apprenticing you this year.

DAEDALUS. Deadline. There's a deadline on this, Icarus, I can't—do you have string?

ICARUS *(fishing the string from his tunic)*. I think you're afraid I'll steal your ideas. You're afraid of your own son. Just like King Minos.

DAEDALUS *(using the string to measure part of the sketch).* No...what I'm afraid of...is that you're right, and King Minos can't be trusted and the sooner we're out of here the better and that's not a problem because I'm done. *(He holds up his drawing.)*

ICARUS. Already?!

DAEDALUS. Simple, really. A series of concentric circles broken up at 15- and 21-foot intervals with 31-degree slopes to disorient the inhabitant and seven hallways running perpendicular to the circles at fractured angles.

ICARUS. It looks like a maze.

DAEDALUS. Labyrinth. I'd call it a labyrinth. Prettier word. Labyrinth.

(MINOS storms back on.)

DAEDALUS *(cont'd).* Ah. King Minos. *(Handing him the plan.)* Your labyrinth.

MINOS. Looks like a maze.

DAEDALUS. Maze, yes. A huge maze to be built beneath your palace. Just put your son—put the Minotaur in at this location and he'll wander forever. Just leave him enough food. And water. Satisfactory?

(MINOS turns the plan over and over, squinting at it, then...)

MINOS. Brilliant! We begin work immediately! You truly are the greatest architect in the world.

DAEDALUS. But not, ah, not the wealthiest. Which you can take steps to remedy, yes? I believe we agreed—

MINOS. Absolutely! As long as you're here, what's mine is yours.

DAEDALUS. We, ah, very generous, very kind, but we need to be leaving—we're designing a theater in Greece, the Epidaurus, and I need—

MINOS. You can design theaters here.

ICARUS. It's not the same.

DAEDALUS. If we could have something portable—gold, perhaps—we'll be on our, as it were, way—

MINOS. That is not going to happen.

DAEDALUS. Ah. *(Pause.)* If one were to ask, hypothetically, why not—

MINOS. One would receive the answer that I need you. Greece doesn't.

DAEDALUS. Debatable, debatable. We'll debate in on our boat— *(Collecting ICARUS.)* Come, my boy, let's...debate...on—

MINOS. Halt! *(They do.)* I don't believe you understand. You're not leaving. One: I think you're immensely talented and I want that talent working for the good of Crete and nobody else. And Two: You know the secret of the maze.

DAEDALUS. Labyrinth.

MINOS. Whatever. You alone could tell the world how to escape it. And I can't have that.

DAEDALUS. Ah.

MINOS. I'll set you up the finest workshop on Earth in this room. You can mold the most brilliant trinkets—create tools to take mankind itself to the highest heights, I don't care. But you'll do it from here. Or you won't do it ever again.

(ICARUS breaks for MINOS—ready to pound him into hamburger—but DAEDALUS catches him—pulls him back with all of his strength and knowledge of physics.)

DAEDALUS. No, wouldn't want that—that would be...undesirable.

MINOS. Then I think we have an understanding. I'll have your tools brought up immediately. Welcome to Crete! *(And he exits.)*

ICARUS. Cretins. I told you so. Didn't I tell you so?

DAEDALUS. Please be quiet. Please. Thank you.

ICARUS. If you'd listened to me—

DAEDALUS. I'd have a steel spike in the middle of the labyrinth. So my next project, it seems, is our escape. *(DAEDALUS begins sketching.)*

ICARUS *(peeking out the door)*. Four guards outside the door. I can take them.

DAEDALUS. A dead son is of no use to me.

ICARUS. Why are you always so sure I'll fail?

DAEDALUS. Four trained warriors. One boy studying to be an architect. Get me the string.

ICARUS *(not handing the string)*. Isn't it possible—just possible—that your son might see an opportunity that you don't—that maybe I have a new idea that could work, and that maybe—just maybe—I could make it happen even when my all-knowing father says it's impossible!

DAEDALUS. Hand me the string.

ICARUS. Get your own string. *(Throwing it to the floor.)* I'll find my own way out. And you can follow me. *(Pause. DAEDALUS walks over, collects the string, and goes back to his planning. ICARUS goes to the window.)*

One window. Big enough to get out. But it's a hundred-foot drop to the ground. And he's got guards all along the beach... So just getting to the boat will be an amazing feat. *(Peering up from the window.)* Wall's too smooth to climb. But the seagulls are making a straight shot from the castle to the beach—

DAEDALUS *(looks up from his work)*. Seagulls.

ICARUS *(moving from the window)*. Stones are solid and well-mortared—

DAEDALUS. The birds. The birds, Icarus—

ICARUS. What?

DAEDALUS. The birds. I was thinking tunnels, I was thinking under, but you're thinking over and you're right.

ICARUS. I don't...well. Yes. Over. The birds.

DAEDALUS *(scribbling on a scrap of paper)*. Give this to the guards—materials we'll need.

ICARUS *(taking the paper and reading it)*. Feathers? Forty pounds of feathers? Wax? *(He hands the paper offstage.)*

DAEDALUS. Glue would be nice, be good, but we can't give that secret to Minos, can we?

(ICARUS and DAEDALUS sit down and commence work on an abstract set of wings.

MINOS enters.)

MINOS. Can't give what secret to Minos??

DAEDALUS. Ah, King, Your Royalness, the secret, ah, the secret of the labyrinth. If you knew, you might be tempted, desirous to set your...the Minotaur—free.

MINOS. Not a chance. What's with the feathers?

ICARUS. A quilt!
DAEDALUS *(simultaneously)*. Pillow.

(They look at each other.)

ICARUS. A pillow.
DAEDALUS *(simultaneously)*. Quilt.
DAEDALUS *(cont'd)*. A pillow-quilt. Quilt for your pillow. Keeps it warm so your head, ears, stay warm. While sleeping.
MINOS. It's going to be awfully wide.
DAEDALUS. More than one pillow at a time.
ICARUS. Heat lots of pillows. You'll see.
MINOS. I had rather hoped you'd create something more... grand. But pillow-quilts are a good start. Carry on. *(MINOS exits.)*
ICARUS. Wings, Father.
DAEDALUS *(returning furiously to work)*. You've been studying the birds as I told you?
ICARUS *(working fast)*. Yes.
DAEDALUS. You know their rhythm?
ICARUS. Every wing beat.
DAEDALUS. How to hold your legs back?
ICARUS. Yes.
DAEDALUS. The angle of the neck?
ICARUS. Yes.

(DAEDALUS holds up two of the four magnificent wings, but not outstretched. Not yet.)

ICARUS. Father. Are they going to work?

DAEDALUS. Of course. Everything I've ever built has worked. But I'll go first. Now make sure you're secure—

(They harness ICARUS into the wings, and start with DAEDALUS.)

ICARUS. I'm secure, Father. Let's fly.

DAEDALUS. Once you're over the sea, hold to the middle path. Too close to the water and the moisture will weigh down the feathers—you'll submerge and drown.

ICARUS. Right. Let's do it.

DAEDALUS. Fly too high, too near the sun, and the wax will melt—you'll come apart and shatter in the sea. Hold to the middle path.

ICARUS. Right. Right.

DAEDALUS. Follow my example—

ICARUS. Father. Are you crying?

DAEDALUS *(turning away)*. You're...ah. You're going to be flying out there—alone—guided by your own judgment, there's no way I can...you follow my example, right?

ICARUS. Stay the middle path.

DAEDALUS. Good. Good. *(They step up onto blocks or benches and ready themselves...preparing to fly.)* That's the difference between Minos and me, Icarus. He's locking his son away. I'm setting mine free.

(And he leaps...followed immediately by ICARUS. They plummet—free-falling for seconds...then at the last moment their spread wings catch the wind and they soar

up...up-up-up—now we see the wings in all their glory. ICARUS begins laughing. DAEDALUS smiles.

We hear the wind blowing past them smoothly, gorgeously.)

ICARUS. The guards on the beach! Did you see the guards!

DAEDALUS. They'll have stories to tell tonight.

ICARUS *(swooping)*. Father! It worked! These are the most glorious things you've ever created!

DAEDALUS. Don't look down. Makes you dizzy.

ICARUS. Not me. I want to see it all—the whole world from up here! Are we the first mortals to see the sea from the clouds?

DAEDALUS. Stay focused, Icarus, keep looking ahead— only a few more miles to go—

ICARUS. But I can swoop! Has any man ever swooped like a gull before? And climb...and dive...and...look at me, Father! Look at me! Look at me!

(The wind grows louder—more rushed.)

DAEDALUS. Stay the middle path, Icarus.

ICARUS *(farther away from his father now)*. What? The wind... Like a lark, like an eagle—like a god! Father! We're like gods!

DAEDALUS. What? I can't...you're drifting too far!

ICARUS. I'll catch up with you...but, Father...I can touch the sky...I can fly to the sun and nothing happens, you see? You're not always right! You're a genius, but you're not always right! I can go up and up and up and up...

(The wind is racing—racing.)

DAEDALUS. Icarus! You're going too high!

(A light grows brighter and brighter on ICARUS.)

ICARUS. I can touch Olympus!
DAEDALUS. Icarus! Don't—

(The light is blinding—the wind howling.)

ICARUS. The sun! The first human to touch heaven!! *(Then his wing buckles.)* No— *(He twists himself—trying to regain control.)* No!!! Father! Father!! *(His other wing folds and he plummets, plummets, faster and faster and faster... And vanishes into blackness.)*
DAEDALUS. Icarus!!! *(He freezes in a wide-open flight position.)*

(Beat.

DIONYSUS re-enters.)

DIONYSUS. Swallowed up by the sea. Did he dream too high? You tell me.

(DAEDALUS folds his wings and kneels.)

DIONYSUS *(cont'd)*. Daedalus landed safely in Sicily. He took his wings to an altar for Apollo, offered them to the Sun God...and never left the earth again. So which shatters your life more—to be actually touched by a god—or have your eyes opened to your own god-imitating powers? And which is worth more: a lifetime on the ground or a few seconds at the peak of human experience? Depends on who you ask. Icarus...or Daedalus.

(Lights go out on DIONYSUS watching DAEDALUS who looks deep into the AUDIENCE.)

Theseus and the Minotaur

(We hear a guttural animal growl in the darkness.

Pause. Then THESEUS bursts in—full of himself, of life, of a desire to do what's right.)

THESEUS. Father! Father!

(AEGEUS, the weak old King of Athens, hobbles in.)

AEGEUS. Theseus.

THESEUS. What's going on? A ship with a black sail was just spotted in the harbor, and your subjects are crying in the streets—running home and bolting their doors.

AEGEUS. This is something you best not know of. Go. Lock yourself away for twenty-four hours and it will all be over.

THESEUS. Father. If I'm to rule Athens when you die, then I need to know what I'm getting myself into. What does that ship want with us?

AEGEUS. The boat hails from Crete. I lost a war with them eighteen years ago. To save our city, I had to agree to a terrible ransom. Every nine years we choose seven young men and seven young women by lots and hand them over to King Minos.

THESEUS. What does he do with them?

AEGEUS. We best get ready. The ship will dock soon—

THESEUS *(stopping him)*. What happens to the fourteen?

AEGEUS. I don't know! Nobody does. Because nobody ever returns. There are rumors that the prisoners are locked into a labyrinth with the Minotaur—a horrible twisted beast—half-bull, half-man. What happens to them then...we don't know. We never ask.

THESEUS. Why hasn't anyone ever stood up to break this contract?

AEGEUS. Our army is still too weak. It's only fourteen children, there are thousands of reasons to let it lie. So let it lie, Theseus. It doesn't concern you.

THESEUS. It does. Anything that terrifies an entire city— even for a day—concerns me. I'll put an end to it.

AEGEUS. You cannot! Besides, they are already drawing the names. It is too late.

(THESEUS races to a "balcony" to hear.)

VOICE *(O.S., calling out to the public)*. The sixth male is Endymion of the house of Latmus. The seventh male—

THESEUS *(shouts out)*. Is Theseus of the house of Aegeus! Prince of Athens!

AEGEUS. No!

THESEUS *(calling out)*. I will travel to Crete and break this pact by killing the Minotaur. Never again will the children of Athens be offered as slaves to King Minos and his monster!

(A huge cheer goes up.)

THESEUS *(turning back to AEGEUS)*. They love me. You see, Father. All it takes is a little courage to win back your people.

AEGEUS. This isn't courage. It's suicide. What am I supposed to do when the only heir to my throne is slaughtered in the pits of Crete?

THESEUS. Go to war. Do what's right. Besides, I don't go to be slaughtered. I go to set us free. And survive.

AEGEUS. But—

THESEUS. I've fought dozens of monsters and robbers on my way to your city, Father. This Minotaur can't be much worse than they were.

AEGEUS. Oh, it can be. It can be.

THESEUS. No disrespect, but cowardice got us into this and only bravery will get us out. I'm going to board that ship for Crete, and when I return victorious, then you can tell me what a fool I was. *(He heads out.)*

AEGEUS. Wait! At least let me send some of my warriors with you—together you can—

THESEUS. No. A hero acts alone. Did I need help defeating Procrustes? Or that barbarian Sinis? I alone took this challenge, and it rests on my shoulders. Alone.

AEGEUS. Theseus, take a white sail with you. When the ship returns, raise the white sail and I'll know you live. If I see that the sail is still black, then…I'll pay for your death with my own. I'll watch every day—every hour— from the cliffs over the harbor.

THESEUS. Watch for the white sail, Father. You'll see it soon. *(And he charges out.)*

AEGEUS. Godspeed, my boy…god…speed…

(As he speaks TWO ACTORS raise a huge black cloth that covers the back wall of the stage.

AEGEUS totters out as THESEUS bounds on—now on the deck of the boat as it sails to sea.)

THESEUS *(pounding the deck)*. Can't this boat go any faster? I see the Isle of Crete up ahead—why aren't we there yet? If this Minotaur is half as impatient as I am, then we certainly can't keep him waiting!

(Another YOUNG ATHENIAN man walks up beside THESEUS to view Crete.)

YOUNG ATHENIAN. Theseus?

THESEUS. What?

YOUNG ATHENIAN. I just wanted—all of us, all the prisoners—thank you.

THESEUS. It's nothing. Any one of you could do it. I'm just the loudest.

YOUNG ATHENIAN. If you want any help, we can—

THESEUS. Thank you. But it comes down to me and him.

YOUNG ATHENIAN. Do you really think you can do it? Kill the Minotaur?

THESEUS. Would I be here if I didn't?

YOUNG ATHENIAN. But what about the labyrinth? Even if you kill the Minotaur, they say no one can find their way back out of the labyrinth.

THESEUS. Well, I hadn't actually...how hard can it be?

YOUNG ATHENIAN. Daedalus designed it. It's the most torturous maze ever devised.

THESEUS. Well...I—

YOUNG ATHENIAN. But you've got a plan, right? We're all behind you! Godspeed! *(Exits.)*

THESEUS. ...thank you. The labyrinth. *(Yelling out.)* Why are we sailing so fast? Slow this boat down! Let's enjoy the scenery a little, hah? No rush. No...rush—

(King MINOS enters on the shore, followed by his tender daughter ARIADNE, who wears a simple crown and no shoes.)

THESEUS *(climbing off the ship)*. King Minos, I presume.

MINOS. Are you it?? Where are all the other Athenians??

THESEUS. They're still below deck. Don't worry, they'll be in your dungeons soon enough. I have a request for you, King Minos.

MINOS. A request?? From a prisoner of war??

THESEUS. I want to be the first one thrown into the labyrinth.

ARIADNE. Oh!

MINOS *(to ARIADNE)*. What?

ARIADNE. Nothing, Father. I said "oh."

MINOS *(to THESEUS)*. Are you insane?

THESEUS. Just tired of your injustice. My father has paid your sickening ransom long enough. It ends today.

MINOS. Wait, wait, wait. Your father?

THESEUS. Aegeus, King of Athens.

MINOS. But that would make you—

THESEUS & MINOS. Theseus, Prince of Athens.

ARIADNE. Oh!

MINOS *(to ARIADNE)*. What did you say?

ARIADNE. Nothing, Father. I said "oh."

MINOS *(pulling THESEUS quietly aside)*. Look. I don't know who talked you into this, but I'm going to let you off easy this time. You're obviously brave, probably an idiot, and I don't need to hurt Aegeus any more than I already have. Go home. Become the ruler of Athens. Keep my payments coming and you'll have a long, healthy life, all right?

THESEUS. No.

MINOS. I beg your pardon?

THESEUS *(loudly)*. I won't let you terrorize our city any longer. If that means facing the Minotaur, then I'll do it.

MINOS. Very well. *(To the crowd.)* We'll see how long your bravado lasts when you're standing alone in the pitch blackness of the labyrinth tomorrow morning! Take him away!

THESEUS *(being pulled off)*. I'll gladly stand alone for my city! Be warned, King of Crete—if I defeat your monster, Athens is free of all debts to you! And if I die, I die—but at least I'll have stood up to your cruelty and corruption! *(And he's gone.)*

MINOS. Words, words, words. We'll see what words you think of when the Minotaur pulls your arm from its socket. *(He starts to leave.)*

ARIADNE. Father?

MINOS. What??

ARIADNE. He is brave. He's honorable. Couldn't you at least give him a sword to make it a fair battle?

MINOS. What are you—Athenian?

ARIADNE. He's just different from the others. And you know how I feel about the Minotaur in the first place—

MINOS. Ariadne, I have got a splitting headache. The last thing I need is for my daughter to stand here yapping at me to spare some fool's worthless life—

ARIADNE. I'm not yapping—

MINOS. Enough! Are you King? No! Will you ever be? No! You're lucky to be Princess! Guards—throw all the Athenians in the dungeons! Theseus goes in at dawn!! *(He storms off.)*

ARIADNE *(quietly).* "Lucky to be Princess." *(She hurries off.)*

(Lights go very dark.

THESEUS is shoved on and tumbles to the floor of his cell. He glowers at the darkness.)

THESEUS *(quietly).* I can do this. I can do this—

(In runs ARIADNE—her crown catching what light there is and looking angelic.)

ARIADNE. Theseus.

THESEUS. Who's there?

ARIADNE. My name is Ariadne. I'm King Minos' daughter.

THESEUS. Just then—seeing you in silhouette—your crown—you looked like…a goddess.

ARIADNE. No. Not a goddess. Just someone who thinks your bravery shouldn't be lost to the world. I've got the keys to your cell. I can free you and all of the prisoners, but you have to take me back with you—

THESEUS. No.

ARIADNE. What?

THESEUS. I can't leave. Not until I've killed the Minotaur and avenged all the children he's slain.

ARIADNE. But that's impossible, Theseus!

THESEUS. Nothing's impossible. Just improbable. I'll find a way.

ARIADNE. Then here. *(She holds out a small sword.)* At least take this sword. Make it a fair fight. *(THESEUS hesitates.)* Don't be a fool. I'm trying to help you!

THESEUS. But a hero finds his own way—acts alone—

ARIADNE. You'll be alone, believe me. There's no way I'm going into that labyrinth. But I know how to get out of it.

THESEUS. You do??

ARIADNE. When I was a little girl, I saw Daedalus once before he fled. He whispered to me. And I've told no one. Until now.

THESEUS. Tell me.

ARIADNE. Gladly...but...how is this different than giving you the sword? I thought you wanted to act alone in this.

THESEUS. I do. I will. But, as you say, I alone will be using the information you give me. And the sword. Thank you.

ARIADNE. Promise to take me back with you when you flee. My father will kill me if he discovers—

THESEUS. I promise. We'll all sail free when I've ended the reign of this monster.

ARIADNE. Then...here. *(She produces a ball of thick twine.)*

THESEUS. String? You're arming me with string?

ARIADNE. For the labyrinth, Theseus. Tie one end to the entrance, and play it out behind you as you twist and turn. Then if—when—you kill the Minotaur, follow it back to me.

THESEUS. Ah.

ARIADNE. But you absolutely have to kill the Minotaur. If he kills you and follows the twine back, he'll be free to destroy the whole island, no one will be safe—

THESEUS. I'll kill him. No fears. *(Kisses her hand.)* Show me this labyrinth.

(They walk to the edge of the stage and THESEUS ties one end of the twine to a pole.

Lights dim even more.)

ARIADNE. Move swiftly. At daybreak, they'll come for you in your cell. We must be far out to sea by then.

THESEUS. I'll move with the speed of the gods.

ARIADNE. Theseus, they say the thing has the body of a huge man—sweating, muscled, matted with hair. He stands seven or eight feet tall. And on his neck and shoulders—as if sewn on by a demon—is the hulking head of a bull. Dead black eyes staring out under the twisted horns and rotting teeth worn into knife points, constantly frothing and drooling. He'll destroy anything that gets in his way.

THESEUS. Not me. Not this time.

(She nods, holding back tears.)

ARIADNE. I'll wait for you here.

THESEUS. Thank you.

(She steps out of sight.

THESEUS turns to face the empty dark stage, sword in one hand and twine in the other. He inches out into the space...a few steps more...then he moves quickly across the stage—attaching the twine to another pole—and moves back in the other direction—scanning the emptiness—moving in yet another direction—creating a maze of his own with the twine.

He pauses...starts to move... CRUNCH!! A huge crash from offstage. He spins to face it...a low growl echoes over the stage. He turns to see where it's coming from—drops the twine—starts to move... WHAMM!! From the other side of the stage! He freezes—terrified—ready for anything...another growl...where's it coming from?? A pounding begins offstage—rhythmic—almost a heartbeat—the lights begin to throb in rhythm with the pounding... Another growl...THESEUS spins—sword ready—pounding grows louder—faster—lights strobing—blinding—deafening—he's about to explode...where...is it... coming from... He spins to face the AUDIENCE... RRROAARRRR!!! The thunderous Minotaur scream BLASTS over everything in a blinding flash of light—THESEUS screams out a battle cry—his voice melting into the animal howl—raises his sword—charges for us— Screammmmmsss...

Silence. Darkness. A long pause. Then footsteps—fast, stumbling—and ARIADNE's quiet terrified whisper.)

ARIADNE. Theseus? Theseus, is that you?

(Desperate movement in the dim, dim light—THESEUS scrambling back along his trail of string—madly grabbing it back up—and leading back to...ARIADNE.

Lights come up slightly as he collapses into her arms. Note: If possible, he and his sword should be soaked in blood.)

ARIADNE. Theseus! You're alive! You're alive— you're ...you did it! You killed the Minotaur!
THESEUS. I killed...the Minotaur...I...
ARIADNE. I knew you could do it. I knew it, I knew it— *(Wrapping a cloak around him.)* Hurry. Hurry! Come on.

(He stumbles onto the ship as the lights come up. The huge black sail continues to loom over the back wall.

The YOUNG ATHENIAN runs in, as THESEUS continues to stare straight ahead.)

YOUNG ATHENIAN. We're away, Theseus. No sign of pursuit. *(He exits.)*

(ARIADNE stands on one side of the stage looking at THESEUS who sits crumpled on the other.)

ARIADNE. I'd say we have about a three-hour lead over them. Theseus. *(He doesn't respond.)* Theseus. Look at me. *(He doesn't respond.)* Theseus. What happened in there?

(Pause.)

THESEUS. I was lucky. It could just as easily be me lying dead down there right now...

(Pause.)

ARIADNE. Go on.
THESEUS. That's all.
ARIADNE. You can tell me—
THESEUS. I said that's all.

(Pause, as they look at each other...

Then the YOUNG ATHENIAN charges back on.)

YOUNG ATHENIAN. Theseus, you've saved the entire city. You're the greatest hero Athens has ever seen! *(THESEUS nods—staring straight ahead.)* And you were true to your word. You did it alone. When push came to shove you were alone and you slew the Minotaur and escaped the labyrinth. How did you do it?

(THESEUS and ARIADNE look at each other. She tries to smile.)

THESEUS. What is that island up ahead?
YOUNG ATHENIAN. It's Naxos.
THESEUS. Let's port there. We're far enough ahead, I think we can rest for a few hours.
YOUNG ATHENIAN. Good thinking. *(Calling off.)* Hard astern! *(He exits.)*

ARIADNE. Are you sure? My father's fleet is—

THESEUS. I'm in charge of this ship. Not you. Me. And I say we land on Naxos.

(The ship lands and THESEUS steps off.)

ARIADNE. Theseus? What will you tell them about how you escaped the labyrinth?

THESEUS. You need rest, Ariadne. I need rest. Go ashore. *(She looks at him. Nods. And exits to sleep.)* A hero stands alone...

(The YOUNG ATHENIAN races on.)

YOUNG ATHENIAN. Theseus! Baucis says he sees a sail on the horizon!

THESEUS. What? Where?

YOUNG ATHENIAN. South. Coming from Crete.

THESEUS. Full sail to the north! Go! Go! Where's Ariadne?

YOUNG ATHENIAN. You sent her ashore.

THESEUS. She's still on the island?

YOUNG ATHENIAN. We've got to turn around—

THESEUS. We can't.

YOUNG ATHENIAN. What?

THESEUS. Keep sailing. We can't go back.

YOUNG ATHENIAN. But—

THESEUS. We don't go back. *(YOUNG ATHENIAN hesitates.)* That's an order.

(YOUNG ATHENIAN nods and runs out.

AEGEUS enters from a far corner, staring out over the sea.)

AEGEUS. Nothing. Every day, every hour...my kingdom grows darker...Theseus...my son—

THESEUS. Land!!

(YOUNG ATHENIAN runs in beside THESEUS.)

YOUNG ATHENIAN. Athens.

THESEUS. We're home.

AEGEUS. Wait. There...a ship—

YOUNG ATHENIAN. I've never seen anything more beautiful in my life—

AEGEUS. But the sail—what color is the sail?

THESEUS. Yes—

AEGEUS. Black.

YOUNG ATHENIAN. Home. Alive and home!

AEGEUS. Dead. My one light put out so quickly after it was struck—

THESEUS. Wait...the sail! Put up the white sail!

YOUNG ATHENIAN. What?

AEGEUS. Then let me die with him. *(Lights go out on AEGEUS.)*

THESEUS. Tear down the black sail—tear it— *(And we hear the scream of AEGEUS throwing himself to his death on the rocks below.)* Father!!

(THESEUS and the YOUNG ATHENIAN freeze as DIO-NYSUS walks out onto the deck of the ship.)

DIONYSUS. Let us leave poor Theseus here. Frozen forever in the moment of his greatest triumph and tragedy. *(THESEUS and the YOUNG ATHENIAN stay frozen.)* Why didn't he raise the white sail? Why did he leave Ariadne behind? I leave those questions for your minds to ponder. My time here is almost done. The moment when my world touches yours is fading fast. *(The opening music begins to play.)*
    THE RUINS RETURN TO SILENCE NOW
    OUR CEREMONIES END
    LET ALL BEHOLD
    AS STONES GROW COLD
    AND ANCIENT GODS ASCEND

(All the ACTORS re-enter as the living STATUES they were at the top of the show—moving slowly into place—chanting/singing…)

ALL.
    LET ALL BEHOLD
    AS STONES GROW COLD…
    AND ANCIENT GODS…
    ASCEND.

(They all freeze in their poses…

Blackout.

And we hear the whispering laugh of the god DIONYSUS…)

END OF PLAY

DIRECTOR'S NOTES